A Twist in the Tale

Five Short Stories

ARTHUR HOEY DAVIS, JOHN GEORGE LANG,
MARY FORTUNE, HENRY LAWSON and
JESSIE COUVREUR

Level 5

Retold by Penny Cameron
Series Editors: Andy Hopkins and Jocelyn Potter

Pearson Education Limited
Edinburgh Gate, Harlow,
Essex CM20 2JE, England
and Associated Companies throughout the world.

ISBN 0 582 41816 X

Dad and the Donovans was first published in 1889, *The Ghost upon the Rail*
was first published in 1859, *The Dead Witness; or, The Bush Waterhole*
was first published in 1866, *Brighten's Sister-in-law* was first published
in 1901, *An Old-Time Episode in Tasmania* was published in 1891
This adaptation first published by Penguin Books 1994
Published by Addison Wesley Longman Limited and Penguin Books Ltd. 1998
New edition first published 1999
Third impression 2000

Text copyright © Penelope Cameron 1994
Illustrations copyright © Bob Harvey 1994
All rights reserved

The moral right of the adapter and of the illustrator has been asserted

Typeset by Digital Type, London
Set in 11/14pt Bembo
Printed in Spain by Mateu Cromo, S. A. Pinto (Madrid)

Published by Pearson Education Limited in association with
Penguin Books Ltd., both companies being subsidiaries of Pearson Plc

For a complete list of the titles available in the Penguin Readers series please write to your local
Pearson Education office or to: Marketing Department, Penguin Longman Publishing,
5 Bentinck Street, London W1M 5RN.

Contents

Introduction

The Australian bush is always ghostly at night, and the moon played strange tricks. I felt as if a strange horse was behind me. And then I started saying 'Death is riding tonight! . . . Death is racing tonight! . . .'

Australia is a new country − but it is also a very old one. It is a land of mysteries, and a land of many stories.

There are stories of the farmers who have to earn their living in a fierce, dry land. There are stories of murders and of ghosts who will not keep silent. There are stories of the strange understanding that the country people have of life. And there are stories of the first Europeans to live in Australia − ordinary people sent from Britain to a hard, new settlement as prisoners.

These five stories by Australian writers each show a different side of an amazing continent and its strong, inventive people − and each has 'a twist in the tale' . . .

John George Lang (1816-1864) was born in Sydney. He studied law at Cambridge University in England, but he was thrown out for saying disrespectful things about God and religion. After finishing his studies in London, he returned to Australia in 1841 and wrote his first book, *Legends of Australia* (1842). He worked as a lawyer in Calcutta, India, for three years, then travelled widely in Europe, working as a journalist. He also wrote short stories for Charles Dickens's magazines *Household Words* and *All the Year Round*. Lang wrote nine novels. His most important one is generally considered to be *Botany Bay: Or, True Tales of Early Australia* (1859).

Mary Fortune ('Waif Wanderer') (1833?–1910?) was born in Belfast, in Northern Ireland. She was the first woman in Australia to write detective stories. *Dead Witness* was her first mystery story. It is typical of her later work, in which detectives work away from cities in the Australian bush and goldfields, and bodies always appear mysteriously out of lakes or are found in tents and suitcases. Arthur Conan Doyle, who created Sherlock Holmes, probably read Mary Fortune. One of his stories, *De Profundis*, is similar in many ways to *Dead Witness*. A collection of her stories, *The Detective's Album: Tales of the Australian Police*, came out in 1871.

Jessie Couvreur ('Tasma') (1848–97) was born in London, but moved to Hobart, Tasmania in the early 1850s. In 1867 she married Charles Fraser, but she was not happy with her husband because he played with money and chased other women. She left him and the marriage ended in 1883 after a long separation. Two years later she left Tasmania for Belgium, where she married a Belgian politician, Auguste Couvreur. After her second husband's death, in 1894, she wrote for *The Times* newspaper. The first and most famous of Tasma's novels is *Uncle Piper of Piper's Hill* (1889). She wrote six other novels, and a number of short stories which were collected in a book *A Sydney Sovereign and Other Tales* (1890). While other (mostly male) Australian writers of her time wrote about the land, Tasma wrote about life in the city. Her stories are interesting and clever descriptions of life in Melbourne. They are also often about women like herself: innocent young women who marry young, realize that their husbands are not right for them, and fall in love with other men better than their husbands. These women, however, are usually unable to find permanent happiness with their new love.

Henry Lawson (1867–1922) is perhaps Australia's most famous writer. He was born in a tent in New South Wales. His father (a Norwegian sailor and goldminer) and mother (a well-known believer in freedom for women) separated in 1883. He got married in 1896 and went to London in 1900, but his wife had a nervous breakdown and left him. Lawson eventually became an alcoholic. Despite having little education and being deaf from the age of fourteen, Lawson wrote almost 150 stories and a lot of poetry. His stories are typical of Australian writing at the beginning of the twentieth century. Most of them are set in the Australian bush, (or 'outback'). His first collection of stories was produced by his mother in 1894. *Brighten's Sister-in-Law* is from Lawson's famous *Joe Wilson and his Mates* (1901). In these stories, Lawson explores brilliantly the problems of a man and wife who live a hard, lonely life in the bush. But his stories always contain humour. For him, humour is the only way to fight off madness or death.

'Steele Rudd' was the pen name of Arthur Hoey Davis (1868–1935). He was born in Queensland, where he grew up on his father's farm. He left school when he was eleven years old, but eventually had an important job as an official in the government justice department in Brisbane. His stories about the Rudd family first appeared in 1899, and were taken from the experiences of his own family. His stories became immediately popular, which did not please the people at the justice department. They thought that he was not serious about his work, and they told him to leave. Rudd started his own magazine in 1904 and went on to write ten books about the Rudd family. These stories are funny on the surface, but underneath the comedy there is a sense of the cruelty and emptiness of life in the Australian bush. However, despite their great poverty, his characters still manage to enjoy themselves. His stories were later made into films and plays on the radio.

Dad and the Donovans

Dad had gone to look after our best horse, Farmer, who had been sick for four days

A very hot summer afternoon. A heat that curled and dried everything. Mother and Sal ironing, wiping their faces with a towel and telling each other how hot it was. The dog stretched out near the door. A child's hat on the floor – the child out in the sun. Two men on horses approaching the gate.

Dad had gone to look after our best horse, Farmer, who had been sick for four days. Dad had built a covering over him, made of branches, to keep the sun off. Two or three times a day Dad cut grass for Farmer, which the cows ate. Dad carried water to Farmer but he refused to drink it.

◆

This afternoon, as Dad approached his patient, he suddenly put down the bucket of water that he was carrying and ran, shouting angrily. Some large black birds flew away from Farmer and settled on a tree close by.

Dad was excited, and when he saw that one of the animal's eyes was gone and a stream of blood ran down over its nose he sat down and hid his face in his big rough hands.

'*Caw, caw!*' came from the tree.

Dad rose and looked up.

'*Curse* you!' he said. 'You black birds from hell!'

'*Caw, caw, caw!*'

He ran towards the tree as if he wanted to throw it to the ground, and the birds flew away.

Joe arrived.

'Were they hurting him, Dad?'

'Oh, you son of the *Devil*!' he began. 'You worthless dog, you! Look there! Do you see that?' He pointed at the horse. 'Didn't I tell you to look after him? Didn—'

'Yes, Dad.'

'Go away!' And Dad threw a piece of wood at Joe, which hit him on the back as he ran away.

◆

Dad returned to the house, still very angry, swearing to take the gun and shoot Joe. But when he saw two horses tied up to the fence he hesitated and would have gone away again if Mother had not called out that he was wanted. He went in unwillingly.

Red Donovan and his son Mick were there. Donovan was a rich man, although some people said that what he owned did not all properly belong to him. He was a man who knew everything – or imagined he knew everything – from the law to being a horse doctor. People could make money out of farming, he said, if they only knew how to make it – most of them, in Donovan's opinion, didn't know enough to get under a tree when it rained. He was a hard man, never giving more than £10 for a £20 animal, or selling a £10 one for less than £20. And few people knew Donovan better than Dad did, or had been tricked by him more often; but this time Dad was in no mood to be kind or easy.

He sat down and they talked of crops and the weather, and then Donovan said, 'Have you any cows to sell?'

Dad hadn't. 'But,' he added, 'I can sell you a horse.'

'Which one?' asked Donovan, for he knew the horses as well as Dad did – perhaps better.

'Farmer.'

'How much?'

'Seven pounds.' Now Farmer was worth £14 if he was worth a penny – that is, before he got sick – and Donovan knew it well.

'Seven,' he repeated. 'Give you six.'

Never before had Dad shown himself to be such a good actor. He shook his head and enquired if Donovan would like the horse for nothing.

'Make it six and a half.'

Dad rose and looked out of the window.

'There he is now,' he said sadly, 'down near the river.'

'Well, what's it to be – six and half pounds or nothing?' asked Donovan.

'All right, then,' Dad replied, 'take him!'

The money was paid there and then and receipts written. Then, saying that Mick would come for the horse on the day following, and after offering a little free advice, the Donovans left.

◆

Mick came the next day and Dad showed him Farmer. He wasn't dead, because when Joe sat on him he moved. 'There he is,' said Dad, grinning.

Mick remained seated on his horse, staring first at Farmer, then at Dad.

'Well?' Dad remarked, still grinning.

Then Mick spoke with feeling. *'You old thief!'* he said, and rode away quickly. It was a good thing for him that he left so fast.

For long after that we put the horses and cows into the little paddock at night, and if ever the dog barked Dad jumped up and ran out in his shirt.

We put them back in the big paddock again, and the first night they were there two cows got out and went away, taking with them the rope that tied up the gate. We never saw them again, but Dad remembered them in his heart. Often, he would think out plans for getting revenge on the Donovans – we knew it was the Donovans. Then the Donovans got into 'trouble' and were reported to be in prison. That pleased Dad; but the revenge was a little indirect. He wanted to catch them.

Four years passed. It was after supper and we were all working by lamplight. Old Anderson and young Tom and Mrs Maloney were helping us. We were going to help them the next week.

Mrs Maloney was arguing with Anderson when the dogs started barking loudly. Dad went out into the dark night. He told the dogs to be quiet, and they barked louder. Then a voice from the darkness said, 'Is that you, Mr Rudd?'

Dad failed to recognize it and went to the fence where the visitor was. He remained there talking for a full half-hour. Then he returned and said it was the young Donovan.

'*Donovan? Mick* Donovan?' asked Anderson. And Mother and Mrs Maloney and Joe echoed, '*Mick* Donovan?' They *were* surprised.

'He's not very welcome,' said Anderson, thinking of his horses and cows. Mother agreed with him, while Mrs Maloney repeated over and over again that she had thought that Mick Donovan was in prison with his bad old father. Dad didn't say much. There was something on his mind. He waited till the visitor had gone, then talked with Dave.

They were outside in the dark. Dad said in a low voice, 'He's come a hundred miles today, 'n' his horse is exhausted, 'n' he wants to take one on his way tomorrow. He wants to leave this one here. What do you think?'

Dave seemed to think rather a lot; he said nothing.

'Now,' continued Dad, 'it's my opinion the horse isn't his; it's one he's stolen – and I have an idea.' Then he went on to instruct Dave in the idea. Then Dad called Joe and taught him the idea too.

That night young Donovan stayed at the house. In the morning Dad was very kind. He asked Donovan to come and show him his horse, as he must see it before thinking of taking it. They went to the paddock together. The horse was standing under a tree, looking tired. Dad stood and looked at Donovan for fully half a minute without speaking. Then he said, 'That's *my own horse* . . .'

Donovan told him he was making a mistake.

'Mistake?' Dad asked, walking round the horse. 'There's no mistake here.'

Just then Dave appeared, as was planned.

'Do you know this horse?' Dad asked him.

'Yes, of course,' he answered, surprised, with his eyes open wide.

'There you are!' said Dad, grinning happily.

Donovan seemed uncomfortable.

Joe in his turn appeared. Dad put the same question to him. Of course Joe knew the horse – 'the one that got stolen'.

There was a silence.

'Now,' said Dad, looking very serious, 'what have you got to say? Who did you get him from? Show us your receipt.'

Donovan had nothing to say; he preferred to be silent.

'Then,' Dad went on, 'go away as fast as you can, and think yourself lucky!'

Donovan went away, but on foot.

Dad looked after him and, as he left the paddock, said, 'I was too clever for you that time, Mick Donovan!' Then to Dave, who was still looking at the horse, 'He's a stolen one right enough, but he's a beauty, and we'll keep him. If the owner ever comes for him, well – if he *is* the owner – he can have him, that's all.'

◆

We had the horse for eighteen months or more. One day Dad rode him to town. He was no sooner there than a man came up and said that he owned the horse. Dad protested. The man went off and brought a policeman. 'All right!' Dad said, '*take* him!' The policeman took him. He took Dad too. The lawyer got Dad off; but it cost us five bags of potatoes. Dad didn't care, because he thought we'd had good value. Besides, he was even with the Donovans for the two cows.

The Ghost upon the Rail

Chapter 1

It was a winter's night – an Australian winter's night – in the middle of July, when two rich farmers in the district of Penrith, New South Wales, sat over the fire of a public house about a mile from their homes. The name of the one was John Fisher and of the other Edward Smith. Both of these farmers had been sent to Australia as convicts, become free men and done well. People said that Fisher had a considerable amount of money, as well as having several houses in the town of Sydney and owning the farm on which he lived. Smith was also in good circumstances resulting from his own hard work, although he had not saved much money.

'Why don't you go home, John, and see your friends and relations?' asked Smith. 'I'm sure they would be glad to see you.'

'I don't know about that, friend,' replied Fisher. 'None of my brothers and sisters have ever answered one of my letters.'

'Did you tell them you were a rich man?'

'No, but I don't think they would care about that much. They are far from rich, but as small farmers they are in a very respectable position in the country. If I was to go back they would be sorry to see me, even if I brought £100,000, because I was once a convict.'

'You don't know people like I do,' Smith said. 'Money changes things, depend on it. Besides, who is to know anything about you, except your own family? And they would never go and hint that you had been unfortunate. How many years ago is it?'

'Let me see. I was then eighteen, and I am now forty-six – twenty-eight years ago. When I threw the stone at the man I didn't think it would hit him, much less kill him. I never thought to be sent here . . .'

It was a winter's night, an Australian winter's night, when two rich farmers sat over the fire of a public house.

'I think you should go home, John. You're always talking of your relations. As for the farm, I'll manage that for you while you're away.'

'Thank you, Ned, I'll think about it.'

The owner of the public house entered the room, and Smith said to him, 'What do you think, Mr Dean? Here is Mr Fisher going back to England, to see his friends and relations.'

'Is that true, Mr Fisher?' asked Mr Dean.

'Oh, yes,' was Fisher's reply.

'And when are you thinking of going?' Dean asked.

'I'm not sure,' Fisher replied, smiling. 'When I'm gone you will hear of it, not before; and neighbour Smith here, who is to manage the farm during my absence, will come and pay you any debt I may leave behind.'

'But I hope you'll come and say goodbye,' said Dean.

'Oh, of course,' said Fisher, laughing. 'If I don't, you can be sure you'll know the reason why.'

After a short while the two farmers departed. Their farms were next to each other, and the two men were old friends.

About six weeks after this conversation Smith called one morning at the public house, informed Dean that Fisher had gone, and offered to pay any amount he owed. Dean remarked that he was sorry that Mr Fisher had not come to say goodbye. Mr Smith explained that Mr Fisher had very good reasons for keeping his departure a secret until after he had left, and hinted that one of Mr Fisher's main reasons for leaving so quietly was to prevent being annoyed by a woman who wanted to marry him.

'Ah! I see,' said Dean. 'And that's what he must have meant that night when he said, "*If* I don't, you'll know the reason why."'

'I miss him very much,' said Smith, 'for when we did not come here to spend our evenings, he came to my house, or I went to his. He gave me an official paper so I can do business for him, and

12

I've got to live at his house while he's away. When he comes back in a couple of years I'm going home to England, and he will do for me what I'm now doing for him. Between ourselves, Mr Dean, he has gone home to find a wife.'

'Indeed!' said Mr Dean. Here the conversation ended and Mr Smith went home.

Fisher's sudden departure caused some surprise throughout the district; but when the explanation given by Mr Smith was spread around by Mr Dean, people stopped thinking any more about the matter.

A year passed, and Mr Smith said that he had received a letter from Fisher in which he said he did not intend to return, and that he wished everything he owned to be sold and the money sent to him in England. This letter Mr Smith showed to several people who knew Mr Fisher well, and they all regretted extremely that they would see no more of so good a neighbour.

Mr Smith advertised the farm and all that went with it for sale, also some houses and pieces of land in and near Sydney and Parramatta; and he arranged to pay Fisher's few debts.

Chapter 2

About a month before the day of the sale, an old man, David Weir, who farmed a small piece of land in the Penrith Road, and who took butter, eggs and chickens to Sydney market every week, was returning to his home when he saw, seated on a rail of the fence along the roadside, the well-known form of Mr Fisher. It was very dark, but the figure and the face were as plainly visible as possible. The old man, who was not drunk although he had been drinking at Dean's public house, stopped and called out, 'Hello, Mr Fisher! I thought you were at home in England!'

There was no reply, and the old man, who was impatient to get home, started off again.

'Mother,' said old Weir to his wife, while she was helping him off with his coat, 'I've seen either Mr Fisher or his ghost!'

'Nonsense!' said the old woman. 'You couldn't have seen Mr Fisher, for he is in Old England. You must have imagined it. How long did you stay at Mr Dean's.'

'Do you mean to say I'm drunk, Mother?'

'No, but you have been drinking.'

'Yes, but I can see, and hear, and understand, and I know what I'm doing.'

'Well, then, have your supper and go to bed; and take my advice and say nothing to anybody about this ghost, or you will only get laughed at.'

'But I tell you I saw him plain as plain could be; just as we used to see him sitting sometimes when the day was warm and he had been round looking at his fences to see that they were all right.'

'Yes, very well, tell me about it tomorrow,' said the old woman. 'Since I was up before daylight, and it's now nearly midnight, I feel too tired to listen to a story about a ghost. Did you sell everything well?'

'Yes, and brought back all the money safely. Here it is.' The old man handed over the bag to his wife and went to his bed; not to rest, however, for the ghost had made a great impression on his mind. He lay awake until daylight, when he got up and went to find his wife.

'I tell you I saw that ghost,' said the old man, 'and there's no need for you to laugh at me. If Mr Fisher has not gone away – and I don't think he would have done so without coming to say goodbye to us – I'll talk about this. What would take Fisher to England? England would be no home to him after being so many years in this country. He has told me that many a time.'

'Well, and so he has told me, David. But then, you know, people will change their minds, and you heard what Mr Smith said about that woman?'

'Yes, but I don't believe Smith. I never had a good opinion of that man, for he could never look me straight in the face, and he is too oily a character to please me. If, as I tell you, Mr Fisher is not alive in this country, then that was his ghost that I saw, and someone has murdered him.'

'Be careful what you say, David; and whatever you do, don't offend Mr Smith. Remember, he's a rich man and you're a poor one; and if you say one word against him he may make you pay for it, and that would be a pretty business for people like us who are trying to save just enough to keep themselves when they're no longer able to work.'

'Well, perhaps you're right. But when I tell you that I saw either Mr Fisher or his ghost sitting on that rail, don't laugh at me, because you'll make me angry.'

'Well, I won't laugh at you, although it must have been your imagination, old man. Where was it you saw, or thought you saw, him?'

'You know that cross fence that divides Fisher's land from Smith's?'

'Yes.'

'Well, it was there. I'll tell you what he was dressed in. You know that old brown coat with the big buttons, and that red handkerchief he used to tie round his neck?'

'Yes.'

'Well, that's how he was dressed. He held his hat in his left hand. I was about ten or eleven yards away from him, for the road is broad just there and the fence stands well back.'

The old woman held her tongue and let old David talk all that day and the next about the ghost, without making any remark whatever.

15

Chapter 3

On the following market day in Sydney old David Weir made his way to the city. He did not talk about the ghost. Having sold his butter and eggs, the old man left Sydney at 4 p.m. and at half past ten arrived at Dean's public house, where he rested his horse. He himself had nothing but water to drink.

At a quarter to twelve the old man was about to start on the last part of his journey home when the two men who were going to Penrith asked him for a ride. One of the men worked for a Mr Cox and the other was a policeman. They both knew all the people who lived in the district.

When they came near the place where the old man had seen the ghost, he made the horse walk as slowly as possible and again saw the figure of Mr Fisher seated on the top rail of the fence, just as before.

'Look there!' said old David to the two men. 'What's that?'

'It is a man,' they both replied. 'But how odd! It seems as if the light is shining through him.'

'Yes,' said old David, 'but look at him. What man is it?'

'It's Mr Fisher,' they said together.

'Hold the horse, one of you,' said old David. 'I'll go and speak to him. They say he's at home in England, but I don't believe it.'

The old man, who was as brave as a lion, approached the ghost and stood within a few feet of it. 'Speak!' he cried. 'Don't you know me, sir? I'm David Weir. How did you get that cut on your head? Are you alive or dead, Mr Fisher?'

There was no answer. The old man then stretched out his hand and placed it on what appeared to be Mr Fisher's shoulder, but it was only empty air.

'Something evil has happened,' said the old man. 'I shall mark the place.' And he broke off several branches from a tree near the rail and put them opposite to the place where the ghost was

*The old man, who was as brave as a lion, approached the ghost and
stood within a few feet of it. 'Speak!' he cried.*

sitting. Then he took out his knife and marked the place where the right hand of the ghost was resting.

Chapter 4

When old David Weir arrived home, his wife, who was delighted to see him so calm, asked laughingly if he had seen the ghost again.

'Never mind about that,' said the old man. 'Here, take the money and lock it up while I look after the horse. He's very tired, and I'm not surprised, for the roads are nearly a foot deep in dust. Then get me some supper ready, for I have some business to do.'

'Where are you going?'

'To Mr Cox's. I'll be home in about an hour.'

The old woman said it could wait until morning, but he took no notice and walked away.

Mr Cox was a very rich gentleman and was a magistrate in the district. He was available at all times of the day and night to any person who considered they had business with him. It was past two o'clock in the morning when David Weir arrived at Mr Cox's house. Mr Cox came out and received the old man kindly, and took him into the house. Old David followed the magistrate and told him all he knew about the ghost of Mr Fisher.

'And who was with you the second time you saw the ghost?'

'One is a man named Williams, who works for you. The other is a man named Hamilton.'

'It's very late,' Mr Cox said, 'and Williams may be tired and have gone to bed. Tomorrow morning I'll go with you to the place and look at it. You say that you've marked it, Weir?'

'Yes, sir.'

The old man then left Mr Cox, and Williams returned to his

bed. Mr Cox did not sleep again until a few minutes before sunrise, and then, when he slept for a quarter of an hour, he dreamt of nothing but the ghost sitting on the rail.

Chapter 5

That morning at eight o'clock Mr Cox rode over to Penrith and saw Hamilton, Weir's second witness. Hamilton, like Williams, agreed with everything Weir had said, and added that no one of the group was drunk.

Mr Cox sent for the leader of the black people in the district, a man called Johnny Crook. Crook was famous for being able to follow marks which showed where people had walked. They all went to the place where the ghost had been seen, and Weir had no difficulty in pointing out the exact rail.

Johnny Crook, after examining the rail carefully, pointed to some marks and said, 'White man's blood!' He walked off and the others followed, until they came to a pool of water with a bluish oil on the surface. This water-hole was not on Fisher's land, nor was it on Smith's. When full it was about ten feet deep in the centre, but at the time referred to there was not more than three and a half feet of water in it, and, badly as the animals wanted water, they were not drinking from it. Johnny Crook walked into the water and felt about with his feet. Soon he found a bag of bones.

Although the body was not recognizable, the buttons on the clothes, and the boots, were those which Mr Fisher used to wear. And in the pocket of the trousers was found a knife with the initials 'J.F.' on it. The murderer, whoever it might be, had either forgotten to take away the knife or had left it with the body on purpose, for all the other pockets were turned inside out.

'Well, sir, what do you think of that?' said old Weir to the amazed Mr Cox.

'I scarcely know what to think of it,' was Mr Cox's reply. 'But it's lucky for you, David, that you're a man of such good character that no one would suspect you of anything so evil. But stay here with the body, all of you, until I return. I shall not be away more than an hour. Have you a pair of handcuffs with you, Hamilton?'

'Several pairs, sir,' replied the policeman.

Chapter 6

After leaving the dead body, Mr Cox rode to Fisher's house, in which Mr Smith was now living. Mr Smith received him with respect. Mr Cox asked if he could speak with him for a few minutes. Mr Smith replied, 'Most certainly, sir,' and took his visitor into the best room in the house.

'I have come to speak with you on a matter of business,' said the magistrate. 'Will the farm and the animals be sold to whoever makes the highest offer?'

'Yes, sir.'

'And the buyer must pay cash?'

'Those are Mr Fisher's orders.'

'How much money do you think the farm will bring, including all the animals and everything that is on it?'

'Well, sir, it ought to be worth £1,500.'

'I hear that everything Mr Fisher owned is to be sold.'

'Yes, sir.'

'What will it be worth, do you think, in cash?'

'Not under £12,000, I should say, sir.'

'I believe that Mr Fisher gave you an official paper so you could do business for him. What is the date on it?'

'I'll tell you, sir, in one minute,' and Mr Smith brought the paper and put it into Mr Cox's hand.

Mr Cox did not know Fisher's signature well enough to

recognize it, although he had seen him write. He did, however, know the signatures of the two witnesses, for they were his own lawyers.

'And do you have the letter telling you to sell for cash?'

'Here's the letter, sir,' said Mr Smith.

Mr Cox read the letter carefully. This is what it said:

Dear Sir

I got home all right, and found my friends and relations quite well. I am so happy among them, I shan't return to New South Wales. So sell everything, but only for cash, as I want the money quickly. I'm going to buy a share in a business with it. The house and farm ought to be worth about £17,000. But do your best, and let me have it quick, whatever it is.

Your faithful friend
John Fisher

There was no postmark on the letter. In those days the postage on letters was very high, and it was common for people to send letters with people who were travelling. The letter was signed in the same way as the official paper.

'All this is most satisfactory,' said Mr Cox. 'Is this letter, dated five months ago, the last you have received?'

'Yes, sir. It came by the last ship, and there has not been another one in since.'

'Good morning, Mr Smith.'

'Good morning, sir.'

Chapter 7

Mr Cox was puzzled. The official paper, written so clearly and signed by Fisher before such respectable witnesses, and then the letter written and signed in the same way by the same hand, made it seem that Fisher had gone to England leaving his friend and neighbour in charge of everything he owned. But then there was the dead body! Mr Cox firmly believed it was Fisher.

When he arrived back at the water-hole he gave instructions to take the body to Fisher's house. Mr Smith came out and he looked amazed, but there was nothing in that. The most innocent man in the world would be surprised at such a sight.

'What is this, Mr Cox?' he said.

'The last that I have heard or seen of Mr Fisher,' was the reply.

'Of Mr Fisher, sir!'

'Yes.'

'These were his old clothes,' said Mr Smith. 'Most certainly this was the old suit he used to wear. But as for the body, it can't be his; for he is alive, as you have seen by his letter. He must have given away these old clothes, and someone must have murdered the man to whom he gave them.'

'Do you think he would give away his knife?' said David Weir. 'He had it for more than twelve years, and I often heard him say he would not sell it for £50.'

'Give it away? Yes!' said Smith. 'Didn't he give away a cow?'

'He was a good man, an honest man and a very fair man, but he was not a giving-away man,' David Weir replied.

'And if he gave away these boots,' said Hamilton, 'they fitted the man who got them very well.'

'This man, whoever he is, was murdered. There's no doubt about that,' said Mr Smith, in the coolest manner.

'And that's why poor Fisher's ghost appears,' said old David Weir.

'Fisher's ghost!' said Mr Smith. 'What do you mean, Weir?'

'Why, the ghost that I've seen twice, sitting on the rail.'

'Ghost! You've seen a ghost, have you?' said Mr Smith, giving Mr Cox a very knowing look. 'Well, I've heard that ghosts do visit those who have sent them out of the world, and perhaps Mr Cox has heard the same. Now if I had been you, I'd have held my tongue about a ghost for fear of being taken to prison.'

'Taken to prison? Me? What I've seen I'll talk about. That was the ghost of Mr Fisher, and this is his body.'

'If I were Mr Cox, I'd get the police to take you,' said Mr Smith.

'I won't do that, Mr Smith,' replied Mr Cox. 'Hamilton. Take Mr Smith to the prison in Penrith.'

'For what, sir?' cried Smith.

'You are accused of murder.'

Mr Smith held up his wrists with the look of an innocent man.

Chapter 8

An enquiry was held into the remains found in the water-hole, and Edward Smith was accused of murder. The jury also found that the body from the water-hole was John Fisher.

By chance, the ship in which Fisher was said to have left Sydney was in the harbour. The captain and officers were questioned and asked, 'Did a man named John Fisher go home in your ship?' The reply was 'Yes'. The captain went on to explain that, when the ship was searched to be sure that no convicts were escaping, John Fisher produced his certificate saying that he was now a free man. This certificate included a description of his personal appearance.

'And did the man exactly fit that description?'

'Yes, allowing for his age. The certificate was dated some years before.'

'And during the voyage did he talk about himself?'

'Frequently. He said he was a farmer near Penrith; that he had earned some money, rented a farm, then bought it, and that he had made a lot of money by hard work.'

'Did he ever mention a Mr Smith, a friend of his?'

'Often. He said he had left everything in Mr Smith's hands and that he did not like to sell his farm until he saw how he liked England after being away so long. He also said that if he liked being in England he would have everything sold off, and join a firm in his own country.'

The lawyers who had prepared the official paper, and witnessed it, said that a person calling himself John Fisher, of the district of Penrith, had come to them. After the paper was completed Fisher took it away with him and told the lawyers to make a copy and keep it in their office. He gave them a cheque on the bank of New South Wales. The lawyers said that the man was about forty-six or forty-eight years of age, about five feet eight inches tall and rather heavy. He had light blue eyes, fair hair going grey and a rather reddish nose. This description matched the way Mr Fisher looked at the time he left New South Wales.

The bank showed various letters which it had received from Mr Fisher. They matched the letters Mr Smith said he had received from England.

Opinion about Mr Smith was very much divided. Numbers of people who knew the man thought that he was incapable of committing such a crime. Smith's house was searched in the hope of finding some bloody clothes, but there was nothing there. Smith's letters and papers were well organized, and his notes about Fisher's business were kept entirely separate from his own. Some examples follow:

Sept. 9 – Wrote to Fisher to say P. has paid the money owed.
Sept. 27 – Received £27/10/- from Wilson for one year's rent of Fisher's house in Sydney.
Nov. 12 – Paid Baxter £3/12/- owed by Fisher.

Many people believed that Weir was the murderer. Many others thought that the bones were Fisher and that the man who had murdered him had robbed him of his certificate, as well as the cash and other papers he had with him, and then, pretending to be Fisher, had left Sydney.

Chapter 9

The day of the trial came at last. The court was crowded with persons of every level of society, from the highest to the very lowest. Mr Smith looked extremely calm. When the witnesses spoke, everyone appeared to hold their breath. Smith, who had no lawyer, questioned them all, and spoke to the jury clearly and well.

The judge then spoke. He was the last man in the world to believe in ghosts, but he considered the story to see how likely it was. His comments were rather on Mr Smith's side.

The jury in those days was not taken from the people but from officers in the army. These gentlemen usually did not give much of their minds to the job. Some of them usually sat back and shut their eyes – not to think but to 'rest'. Others whispered to each other about their own business. But in this case they paid attention, in order to be able to arrive at the truth. They listened with breathless attention to every word the judge spoke, and when he had finished they requested permission to retire to consider what they had heard. This was at half past five in the afternoon of Friday, and the jury did not return to court until a quarter to eleven. Then they were asked, 'Gentlemen, what do you say? Is the prisoner guilty or not guilty?'

With a firm, clear voice their leader replied – 'GUILTY!'

From the unwilling way the judge put the black hat on his head it was clear that he was not satisfied with the finding of the jury. However, he could not change it, and in the usual manner he said that the prisoner would be hanged on the following Monday morning at eight o'clock.

Smith listened without moving at all or showing any sort of emotion, and left the court with as firm a step as he used when he entered it. His manner throughout the trial, and afterwards, changed the opinion of many who thought he was guilty but now believed him to be innocent. A letter to the Governor begging him to spare Smith's life was quickly written, and was signed by many. It was said that the judge agreed that Smith should not die, and that the Governor, respecting this opinion, had ordered a letter sparing Smith to be written but not to be delivered until seven o'clock on the Monday morning. It was also said that the Governor thought that Smith was guilty. The newspapers said that it would be like murder to take away the life of any human being after such a trial.

Chapter 10

On the Monday morning Smith was brought out to be hanged. Many people had gathered, and when Smith's hands were being tied the crowd cried out, 'Shame! Shame! Hang Weir! He's the guilty man! This is a murder! A horrible murder!' And when they saw how calmly Smith listened to the priest who was with him for his last minutes on earth, the people shouted louder.

At one minute past eight Smith was hanged, and after struggling for about half a minute he was dead. Then the crowd shouted again. 'Shame! Shame! Shame! Murder! Murder! Murder!' These noises could not bring Mr Smith back to life, and after hanging for an hour his body was taken away to be buried.

Sydney was gloomy until that evening at half past six. Almost everyone now thought that the blood of an innocent man had been spilled. 'The witnesses all lied, and that includes Mr Cox'; 'the jury were fools'; and 'the Governor, who would not listen to the judge, is a hard-hearted and cruel man': such were the opinions from one end of Sydney to the other. But at the hour mentioned – half past six in the evening – it became generally known that Mr Smith had sent for the priest on the night before, and had told him that he deserved to hang. He said that for more than two years he had planned the murder of John Fisher. The man who had pretended to be John Fisher and who had arranged the official paper, gone to England and written from there was a convict who looked like Fisher. Smith said he gave this man Fisher's certificate. It was Smith's plan to leave New South Wales as soon as he received Fisher's money. This was partly because he wanted to spend the last part of his life in England, but mainly because, from the day on which he did the murder, he had seen the ghost which old Weir had seen sitting on the rail. Smith said he killed Fisher with one blow and that he never spoke again. He said that the man who had pretended to be Fisher did not know of Smith's plan to murder Fisher, and that the letter which came from England was only a copy of one which Smith had told the man to send a few months after he arrived home. He finished by saying that since he killed Fisher his life had been worth nothing, and that he would rather die than go on living this way, although he hoped that until the breath left his body his story would be kept a secret.

The Dead Witness; or,
The Bush Water-hole

There are few things more enjoyable than a spring ride through the Australian bush. A good horseman, with an easygoing horse under him and plenty of time to journey through the park-like bush of Australia, has to my mind an excellent opportunity to enjoy the good life. I was just thinking this as I slowly rode through the forest that comes close to the mountains which divide the district of Kooama into two equal parts. I had passed through fifteen miles of bush without seeing a face or a roof, and now, being only a mile or two from the house where I was going, I let my horse take his own time. While, however, I greatly enjoyed the unbroken calm of nature around me, I cannot exactly say that my mind was enjoying the same 'sweetness of doing nothing' as my body. My brain was busily at work, full of professional problems.

These were the facts of the matter: A young photographer, in search of beautiful countryside to take pictures of, had taken a room in a public house in the town of Kooama. Here he arranged his camera and his tools, and perfected the pictures which he had taken in the district. This young man, barely twenty years of age, was gentlemanly and handsome. His kindness to the children of the place made the parents like him; he was a general favourite in Kooama.

Well, one day the young artist, whose name was Edward Willis, left Kooama and did not return. For a day or two the people at the house where he had been staying thought nothing of his absence, as he had on more than one occasion before spent the night away; but day after day passed, and they began to think it odd. He had said he would visit some of the mountains in search of more views for his camera, but nobody really knew where to start looking for him. His decision to leave Kooama, if he had made one, must have been sudden, as nothing was taken from his room. Camera, photographic plates and all the tools of a photographer's work were still lying about just as he had left them. A week passed – a fortnight – taken up in guesses – and then came a letter from his mother in Adelaide saying that they were getting uneasy at not hearing from their son. Then it was considered time to place the thing in the hands of the police, and I was sent for.

I was travelling quietly through the bush, and thinking about this business, when I heard the loud crack of a whip ring out between me and the mountains to my left, and soon afterwards I heard a horse coming closer. The noise echoed and re-echoed off the rocks at either side of the horseman's route. The sound came nearer and nearer, and at last a young man, riding a good horse and dressed like someone who worked on the land, rode up to me.

'Aren't you afraid of breaking your neck, mate,'* I enquired, 'coming down those hills so fast?'

'Not a bit of it,' he replied. 'I'm in a hurry, so I have to risk it.'

'Going to Kooama, I suppose?'

'Yes, I'm going to call the police, and if I don't hurry it'll be dark before I get back, so I must move on. Goodbye! I'll meet you again, I suppose.'

'Stop!' I shouted as the young man rode off. 'I might save you a journey, as I'm a policeman myself, and am just on my way to Kooama. Is anything wrong your way?'

The young man looked at me closely as, of course, I was not in uniform. He probably did not believe me.

'Well,' he said, 'it's nothing very special, and if you're going to the police, policeman or no policeman, you can tell them all I have to say as well as I can, if you'll be so kind, and I shall get home before sunset yet.'

I persuaded him that I really was connected with the police

---

* mate. In Australian language, a male, or, less usually, a female companion. 'Mate' can be used when one man does not know another man's name.

force, and he told me: 'There's been a lot of talk at Kooama about a young photographer who's been missing for a couple of weeks, and some think he's come to a bad end. Now I know that he's been on our land since he came to Kooama, because I saw him taking views over the hills there, but I thought nothing of that. This afternoon, however, the animals were very restless, and I couldn't understand it until I realized they had come across the smell of blood somehow. Sure enough, when I came up they were moving around a place on the grass that must have had a lot of blood on it, because it was red and still fresh-looking. The place had been carefully covered up with branches, and no one would have noticed it. That made me suspect something was wrong. Heaven knows what might have caused it, or whether it's worth mentioning; but it's not far from where I saw the photographer, so I thought I would tell the police about it.'

'Have you mentioned it to anyone else?' I enquired.

'No,' he replied, 'I haven't seen anyone since.'

'Well, don't say a word. It's very strange that I've met you; I'm Brooke, the detective, and I'm on my way to Kooama about exactly this business. Will you meet me at sunrise tomorrow morning, and take me to the place?'

The young man promised, and I found he was the son of the owner of Minarra, a large farm on the other side of the mountain. Then we parted, and soon I reached the police station at Kooama, fed my horse and got my supper, as well as all the information I could from Constable Cassel before I went to bed.

There are a good many people who can go to sleep easily when they have a lot to think about. It is not so with me; I usually carry my worries to bed with me. Despite this I met the young man at the place we had agreed at sunrise, and together we rode to Minarra.

We went over the hills and three or four miles through the forest beyond. Then my companion, who knew the landmarks well, stopped next to what appeared to be a few branches which had fallen from a tree. 'This is it,' he said, removing the dead wood. 'I covered it up again yesterday.'

Well, there was very little to see: an area of blood-coloured grass and nothing more. I looked round to see if it would be worth an artist's time to visit this place, and, indeed, from exactly where we stood a photographer might catch a truly beautiful view. The sun was up above the trees now, and looking at the ground at my feet I noticed something that caught the sun a few yards away. I picked it up; it was a small, a *very* small piece of glass, which was not far from the blood spot on the grass. I found the marks of the camera support. The holes were marked deeper into the grass than the weight of the camera would explain, especially two of them; the third was not so visible. We covered everything up again, and after having told the young man to be silent I left him and made my way back to Kooama.

An hour or so later I had locked myself into the room of the young artist, and I was very busy. I was quite at home among the poor young man's photographic equipment as I am a bit of a photographer myself, and I have often found my knowledge to be useful to my job. The table was covered with unfinished photographic plates. I found one plate, only parts of which had 'come out' and which was worn in places. Edward Willis seemed to have thrown it away as worthless. There were two or three copies of the same view, and one finished copy which was carefully wrapped. It was a truly beautiful bit of completely Australian bush: a steep, rocky bank at the back; at its foot, a still, deep water-hole mirroring every leaf of the old trees that hung over it. It was an excellent picture; every leaf had come out perfectly, and the shadows were as dark and cool as shadows could be. When I compared the unfinished picture with the perfect one, I saw something which made it a hundred times more valuable to me.

An hour or so later I had locked myself into the room of the young artist, and I was very busy.

In the shadows at the opposite side of this still, deep water-hole there was a pale human figure, a picture so weak that probably only the sharp eye of a detective would have seen it. We all know how perfectly the camera can picture things; here I had this evil-looking face looking from behind a tree, as recognizable as if he had been photographed with great care. I completed a likeness quite good enough for my purpose and left the room.

A woman gave me a picture of the missing young man; he had given it to her a few days before he took his last walk in search of subjects for his art. He was very handsome and very young-looking; a white, sickly face with large black eyes, and a lot of curly black hair. I felt sick at heart as I looked at it and thought of his empty home and the red pool of blood on the grass at Minarra.

It was late in the day, and I was rather glad that my young friend did not come to Kooama that evening, for I was likely to need his help and did not want to trust him with my secrets any longer than was necessary.

Early the next morning he rode up. 'I don't know your name, my young friend,' I began.

'My name is Derrick – Thomas Derrick.'

'Well, Mr Derrick, I'm sure I don't need to tell you what a serious job this is. I am going to ask you for your help, and to ask that you will keep secret anything that may pass between us until I have finished.'

The young man promised to keep everything we said secret, and then I laid the picture of the bush water-hole before him.

'Is there any place like this on Minarra?'

'There certainly is.'

'I thought it likely, and now I'm almost certain that you'll be able to tell me who this is,' and I handed him my copy of the hiding figure.

He looked amazed, and replied immediately, 'It's Dick the Devil!'

'And who is Dick the Devil?'

'A bad-tempered old man who keeps sheep for us. Do you think *he's* in it?'

'We don't know yet. Where does this Dick live, and what does he do?'

'He looks after some of our sheep, and lives about ten miles from the big house.'

'Alone? Or has he a companion?'

'Well, he's been by himself for a long time. He's had two or three men with him, but nobody will live with him for more than a few days.'

'Could you manage to get me in there without making him suspect anything?'

'You! Of course I could; he's always complaining about being alone.'

'It won't be for long,' I said.

That same afternoon we went to Dick's small, dirty house. Dick was within sight, letting his sheep feed quietly, and his young employer brought me to him.

'Now, you old complainer, I hope you're satisfied! Here's a mate for you, and I hope you'll keep your ugly temper quiet for a week.'

I would have recognized my man anywhere, sure enough; the evil, angry face of the hider in the photograph was in front of me. He was an elderly man – about fifty, perhaps – short and strongly built.

'Thank you for nothing, Tom,' he said. 'You didn't send to town for a mate for me, I know.'

'Well, you're right. I met him as I was coming over with your food, and as he looked tired and poor I thought I'd give you another chance.' The young man turned to me. 'Well, so long, mate,' he said.

'Well,' said Dick the Devil, 'if you'll give me a hand with the sheep, I'll get 'em in all the sooner, and then we can talk. I'm glad to see a man's face again.'

We started to move the sheep. 'Have you no dog?' I asked.

'No, I haven't,' he said quickly, with a look half of terror and half of surprise. I felt there was a lot more to be learned about his dog.

After we had eaten, Dick and I sat down in the still, calm evening and smoked.

'Things are looking bad in the country now,' Dick said.

I agreed with him. 'I've walked hundreds of miles without the chance of a job.'

'Where did you come from last?'

'Oh! I came from everywhere between here and Beechworth! I stopped at Kooama last night; there's a lot of talk there about some murder!'

'Murder!' said Dick with a short quick look at me. 'What murder?'

'Some poor painter or picture-man, or something of the sort.'

'They don't *know* he's murdered.'

'I see you've heard about it then. Yes, I believe you're right. I think he's only missing, and they guess someone's killed him.'

'Let them guess!' said Dick, and I decided to drop the subject.

I thought to myself, 'If you only knew who I am, and why I'm here, there would be more blood under a tree somewhere.' Then I looked at my neighbour's strong body and wondered if I could win in a fight with him. There wasn't a living person within miles, and not a sound except the cry of the birds as night fell. I was not sorry that Dick showed no wish to keep on talking but soon went to bed. I followed his example, but only after placing my gun under my hand, and when I *did* sleep it was, as the saying is, with one eye open.

Early next morning young Tom Derrick rode up.

'Why are you taking your sheep to the rock water-hole every day, Dick?' he asked. 'Connel complains you don't leave him half enough for his sheep, and there's a water-hole here, right under your nose.'

'Well, the sheep always go up that way, and it's hard work to turn thirsty sheep away from water when you've got no dog. In fact, it's impossible!'

'What have you done with your dog?'

'Done with him!' replied Dick angrily. 'Cut his throat! He was always giving me twice the work.'

'Well, you'll have to get another somewhere; take the sheep to Minarra water-hole in future.'

'I can't by myself,' was the answer.

'Your mate will lend you a hand for a day or two. The water's not far away, and the sheep will soon get used to it.'

I watched Dick carefully while they were talking and I could see he did not like this order. Still, he could make no excuse, and we headed the sheep for Minarra water-hole. The sheep showed no wish to go in any other direction, and when they had satisfied their thirst I approached the water-hole. I sat down in exactly the spot where poor young Willis must have put his camera to take the view I had in my pocket. I began to smoke my pipe. I could see that Dick was very uncomfortable. He kept well away, but when he saw me taking it coolly he came up slowly.

'Odd place to sit down,' he said. 'You'll be eaten up by insects.'

'No fear,' I answered. 'I think the insects have something they like more down here.'

'Down where?'

'In the water. What a lot of ugly things must be down at the bottom there, Dick! It's very deep.'

I didn't dare look at him, nor did I dare to turn my back to him. I got up and faced him as I pretended to search in my pockets for matches, while my hand held my gun.

'I wonder if the picture-man ever took this place?' I added. 'It would look very good.'

Dick's face reddened with anger. 'D— the picture-man!' he shouted. 'What the — are you always talking about *him* for?'

I looked at him with pretended surprise. 'You get very angry over it, mate! Anyone but me would wonder whether you'd done it yourself.'

His face was terrifying. 'If I *did*,' he said, 'you couldn't prove it. You've no witnesses!'

While he was saying this some air rose to the surface of the water in front of us, followed by more and more. I don't know why I did it, but I took Dick by the wrist and said, 'Haven't I? Look!' Of course I had no more idea of the awful thing that happened next than my reader has now.

A fearful, wet *thing* rose to the surface – a white face followed – and then up, up, waist-high out of the water rose the body of the murdered artist!

It remained for a second or two standing, empty eyes turned towards the bank on which we stood, and then, with a horrible sound, the body fell backwards, the feet rose to the top, and there the terrible thing lay, face upwards. Dick the Devil gave a wild cry that I shall never forget, threw both his hands up to his head and fell heavily to the ground.

To tell you how I felt in those few moments is impossible. I was horrified. But it did not last long with me; for, of course, reason soon made me realize that it was natural for a body to rise from the bottom to the top of a water-hole.

I fired off my gun as a signal to young Derrick, and I soon heard in reply the sound of the young man's whip, and it was not long before he arrived at the side of the water-hole.

The young man must have been even more horrified than I was. After I had told him what had happened I do not think we had two opinions about the guilt of Dick the Devil. I put the handcuffs on him while he was unconscious, not wanting to give him a chance to attempt an escape. Then we poured water over him and he sat up, but when he saw the body he struggled to his feet, crying, 'Oh, my God! Take me out of this! Let me out of this!'

And, one on either side of him – he partly leading – we followed him three or four hundred yards, where, under a tree, he sat down as weak as a child.

'I can't go any farther,' he said. He immediately went on, 'I'm going to tell you about it while I'm able, for I feel rotten like – like *him*, down there.'

We did not speak, either of us, and he went on. 'One day that young man came to take pictures up there, and my dog was playing as usual and running the sheep the wrong way, and the dog got me so angry I took out my knife and cut its throat. The young picture-man saw me and ran to try to save the dog; but he was too late, and he told me I was cruel and called me all sorts of names, and when he went away I swore I'd get my revenge. I watched him that day down at Minarra water-hole, but I couldn't get a chance, and then he was back taking photographs there.'

Here he pointed in the direction of the blood marks, and I nodded, saying, 'I know.'

'You know!' he said, turning to me with some of his old anger. 'How do you know anything about it?'

'I know all about it,' I said in reply. 'I will finish your story for you – when I go wrong, you can put me right.'

He looked at me stupidly – wonderingly. 'Who are you?' he asked.

'I'm Brooke, the detective.'

'Oh!' Dick the Devil took a deep breath.

'Well, he was taking views with his camera near that tree there, where you covered the blood up with the branches – you know, and you went up behind him –'

'Yes,' said Dick, 'when his head was under that black cloth.'

'And you hit him with a piece of wood, and the blow hit the camera too, and it fell and broke.'

39

'Right!' said Dick, looking pleased with himself. 'And then I took out my knife and cut his throat, just as I did the dog's, and I asked him how he liked it, but he couldn't tell me!'

'Oh, you *awful* devil!' cried young Derrick, looking pale and sick.

'And then I carried him all the way to the water-hole on my back,' Dick went on. 'I got a rope and I tied it to a good-sized stone, and I rolled him and the stone to the bottom together! But tell me now,' he added, sinking his voice to a whisper, 'how did he get up again? How *ever* did he get up again?'

Of course we can only guess the answer to Dick the Devil's question. Perhaps the rope was damaged when the body and rope rolled down the bank, and remained tied to the feet. Perhaps the rope then stretched until the body was able to break the surface. This is the most likely explanation, for when we took the body from the water-hole we found the rope was still tied to both the body and the rock.

Dick the Devil was punished for his crime, but where and when it is unnecessary for me to say.

Brighten's Sister-in-law

Mary and I had been married about two years when Jim was born. We called him Jim from the first because Jim was a popular bush name, and most of my old mates were Jims.

We lived in an old house in Gulgong, and I did any sort of work I could find, just to keep food on the table. It was a hard life, but we had Jim, and everything went well for him until he started cutting his teeth. And then Jim started having convulsions.

Did you ever see a child in convulsions? You wouldn't want to see it again: it plays the devil with a man's nerves. I remember the first time very well. I'd got the kettle on the fire – I was going to make some tea and put a piece of beef on to boil overnight – when Jim screamed out twice. He'd been crying a lot, and I was tired and worried (over some money a man owed me) or I'd have noticed at once that there was something unusual in the way the child cried out. As it was I didn't turn around until Mary screamed 'Joe! Joe!' You know how a woman cries out when her child is in danger or dying – short, and sharp, and terrible. 'Joe! Look! look! Oh, my God, our child! Get the bath quick! quick! It's convulsions!'

Jim was bent right back, and he was completely stiff, and his eyes were turned back into his head so you could only see the whites – a thing I saw twice afterwards and I don't want ever to see again.

I was falling over things, getting the bath and the hot water, when the woman who lived next door rushed in. She called to her husband to run for the doctor, and before the doctor came she and Mary had got Jim into a hot bath and saved him.

The neighbour woman made me a bed in another room, and she stayed with Mary that night; but it was a long time before I got Jim's and Mary's screams out of my head and fell asleep.

You can be sure I kept the fire burning and a bucket of water

42

Mary screamed 'Joe! Joe!' You know how a woman cries out when her child is in danger or dying — short, and sharp, and terrible.

hot over it for a good many nights after that; but (it always happens like this) there came a night when I was too tired to think about the fire, and that night Jim took us by surprise. Our wood was done, and I broke a new chair to get a fire and had to run a quarter of a mile for water; but this convulsion wasn't as bad as the first, and Jim came through it.

You never saw a child in convulsions? Well, you don't want to. It must only be a matter of seconds, but it seems long minutes; and half an hour afterwards the child might be laughing and playing with you, or stretched out dead. It upset me a lot. I was always easily upset, and after Jim had his first attack, every time he cried, or turned over, or stretched out in the night, I used to jump. I was always feeling his head to see if he was feverish. Mary and I often laughed about it – afterwards. I tried sleeping in another room, but I kept thinking I could hear them screaming again, and I used to rush into their room and find them sleeping peacefully. For the first few nights I was like that all night, and I was always glad when daylight came. I was in first thing to see they were all right; then I'd sleep until midday if it was Sunday or I had no work. I wasn't very well: I was worried about some money for a building I put up and never got paid for; besides, I was rather wild before I met Mary.

I was fighting hard then – struggling for something better. Mary and I were born to better things, and that's what made the life so hard for us.

Jim got on all right for a while, but his teeth kept holding him back. Just as he was getting fat and happy, another tooth came along, and soon he was thin and weak and big-eyed again. But he was a great little boy. When he was two he was everybody's favourite. I had my own ideas about bringing up a child. I thought Mary was too soft with Jim. She'd say, 'Put that' (whatever it was) 'out of Jim's way, will you, Joe?' and I'd say, 'No! leave it there, and make him understand he's not to have it. Make him have his meals without any nonsense and go to bed at a regular hour,' I'd say. Mary and I had many an argument over Jim. She'd say that I forgot he was only a baby; but I held that a baby could be trained from the first week, and I believe I was right.

I was very fond of Jim, and we were great mates. Sometimes I sat and wondered what he was thinking about, and often, the way he talked, he made me uneasy. If I got my hair cut, he wanted his cut too; and it always worried him to see me shave – as if he thought there must be something wrong somewhere because he wasn't shaving too. I put soap on him one day and pretended to shave him, but it didn't quite satisfy him. He felt his face, looked very hard at the soap I shaved off and complained, 'No blood, Daddy!' (I used to cut myself quite often: I was always impatient over shaving.)

Mary understood what he was saying better than I did. I wasn't always comfortable with him. Sometimes he sat looking into the fire, with his head on one side, and I used to watch him and wonder what he was thinking about, until he seemed at least twenty years older than me; sometimes, when I moved or spoke, he used to look round as if he wondered what his old fool of a father was doing now.

I got a big job building the fence along the front of a ten-mile paddock, near Gulgong, and did well out of it. The railway had got as far as the Cudgegong River – about twenty miles from Gulgong and two hundred from the coast. A man could make good money carrying things from the railway to wherever they were needed. I had two strong horses, and a couple more out in the bush. I bought an old wagon and started carrying from the railway through Gulgong and along the bush roads to the lonely farms. They were a mixed lot of horses, none very good, and I looked after all the equipment myself.

Before this, whenever I made a few pounds I used to go looking for gold, but Mary never let me rest until she had talked me out of that.

I decided to take on a small farm near Lahey's River. I could see it would be a safe place for Mary and Jim, but I was afraid to move out there because I had to be close to a doctor or a good woman neighbour. Then other people started settling at Lahey's River, and it was the time to settle on our place. Mary's married sister was living in Gulgong, and she looked after Jim while we were moving on to the farm. Then I got a small job carrying some flour from Gulgong to Lahey's River. The roads were good, the weather fine, there was no chance of it raining, and I decided to take Jim home with me.

Jim was turning three then, and he was such a little old man he made me laugh. It worried me, too. He always seemed too old for his years. Jim was intelligent for his age, and I often told Mary that he was learning too much from the people who came to our house.

I don't believe in parents talking about their own children all the time – you get sick of it – but I really do think that Jim, when he was three years old, was the most wonderful little boy, in every way, that I ever saw.

For about the first hour, all along the road, he was telling me about his adventures at his aunt's.

'But they spoilt me too much, Dad,' he said, 'and besides, a boy should stay with his parents.'

I was taking out a young dog for a man I knew, and it took up a lot of Jim's attention that day.

Sometimes he surprised me, the way he talked; and other times I had to turn my head away, or cough, or shout at the horses to keep from laughing. And once he said, 'Why don't you tell me something?'

'Tell you what, Jim?'

'Tell me some talk.'

So I told him all the talk I could think of. Then he said, 'I'm glad you took me home with you, Dad. You'll get to know Jim.'

'What!' I said.

'You'll get to know Jim.'

'But don't I know you already?'

'No, you don't. You never have time to know Jim at home.'

And, looking back, I saw that it was cruelly true. I had known in my heart all along that this was the truth, but it came to me like a blow from Jim. You see, it had been a hard struggle for the last year or so; and when I was home for a day or two I was generally too busy, or too tired and worried, or full of plans for the future to take much notice of Jim. Mary used to speak to me about it sometimes. 'You never take notice of the child,' she used to say. 'You could surely find a few minutes in the evening. What's the use of always worrying? You'll be an old man, and Jim a young one, before you realize that you had a child once. Then it will be too late.'

This sort of talk from Mary always made me impatient, because I knew it all too well. I never worried for myself – only for Mary and the child. And often, as the days went by, I said to myself, 'I'll take more notice of Jim and give Mary more of my time, just as soon as I can see things a bit clear for the future.' And the hard days went on, and the weeks, and the months, and the years – Ah, well!

Mary used to say, 'Why don't you talk to me, Joe? Why don't you tell me your thoughts, instead of shutting yourself up in yourself and worrying – eating your heart out? It's hard for me: I get to think you're tired of me, and selfish. I might be angry and speak sharply to you when you're in trouble. How am I to know, if you don't tell me?'

But I didn't think she'd understand.

And so, getting to know each other, Jim and I went along the lonely bush road and camped some fifteen minutes before sunset. Jim badly wanted to help me with the horses, but I made him stay well away. It was a good place to stop, and after

I'd made us comfortable I stood back to admire the view.

I looked round and there was Jim (I thought he was playing with the dog). He was standing close beside me, his hands behind his back, his back to the fire.

He held his head a little on one side, and there was such an old, wise expression in his big brown eyes – just as if he'd been a child for a hundred years or so.

'Dad!' he said. 'Dad! Do you think I'll ever grow up to be a man?'

'Wh–why, Jim?' I asked.

'Because I don't want to.'

I couldn't think of anything against this. It made me uneasy. But I remember I used to have a childish fear of growing up to be a man.

I went to get some water for tea. Jim stayed and played with the dog. I started to cook some food, and Jim said, 'Don't cook too much, Dad – I mightn't be hungry.'

I brought him the meal, but he looked too tired to eat. He only took a mouthful or two, and then he said, 'I'm not hungry, Dad. You'll have to eat it all.'

It made me uneasy. He had eaten some fish in Gulgong and I was afraid it was upsetting him.

'Sick, Jim?' I asked.

'No, Dad, I'm not sick. I don't know what's wrong with me.'

'Have some tea, son?'

'Yes, Dad.'

I gave him some tea, with some milk in it I'd brought from his aunt's for him. He took a very little and said, 'Jim's tired, Dad.'

I made him lie down while I fixed up the camp for the night. I made Jim a bed at the end of the wagon and went to get him. He lay back, looking at the stars in a dreamy way I didn't like. Whenever Jim was extra quiet or affectionate there was trouble.

'How do you feel now, son?'

It seemed a minute before he heard me and turned from the stars.

'Jim's better, Dad.' Then he said something like 'The stars are looking at me.' I thought he was half asleep, when he said, 'Kiss me night-night, Daddy.'

I'd rather he hadn't asked me – it was a bad sign. As I was going to the fire he called me back.

'What is it, Jim?'

'Get me my things, and the dog, please, Daddy.'

I was frightened now. His things were some toys and rubbish he'd brought from Gulgong, and I remembered the last time he'd had convulsions he took all his toys and a little cat to bed with him. And 'night-night' and 'Daddy' were two-year-old words to Jim. I'd thought he'd forgotten those words – he seemed to be going back.

'Are you warm enough, Jim?'

'Yes, Dad.'

I started to walk up and down – I always did this when I was extra worried. I was frightened now about Jim, though I tried to hide it from myself. He called me again.

'Take the blankets off me, Father, Jim's sick!'

I was afraid now. I remembered a neighbour of ours who'd had a little girl die (she swallowed a pin), and when she was going she said, 'Take the blankets off me, Mother – I'm dying.'

And I couldn't get that out of my head.

I felt Jim's head – he seemed cool enough.

'Where do you feel bad, son?'

No answer for a while, and then he said suddenly, in a voice which sounded as though he was talking in his sleep, 'Put my boots on, please, Daddy. I want to go home to Mother.'

I held his hand and he slept in a restless, feverish sort of way. Then I felt him again: his head was burning hot and his skin was dry as a bone. I lost my nerve and started running backwards and forwards between the wagon and the fire, and repeating what I'd heard Mary say the last time we had fought for Jim: 'God! don't take my child! God! don't take my boy!' I wanted a doctor badly, but the nearest one was fifteen miles away.

I looked up at the branches in desperation; and, well, I don't ask you to believe this, although most old bushmen will believe anything in the bush by night; and it might have been a bit of the sky, or the smoke … but I saw the figure of a woman, all in white, come down, down, nearly to the tree, point on up the main road, and then float up and up and disappear, still pointing. I thought Mary was dead! Then I remembered –

A man called Brighten lived four or five miles up the road. He was a small farmer, and his wife was a childish, tired, spiritless woman, and they were both rather strange, worn down by loneliness – they weren't likely to be of any use to me. But I'd heard talk of a sister of Brighten's wife who'd gone out to live with them; she'd been a hospital nurse in the city and there were stories about her. I hoped she was as extraordinary as people said, because I wanted someone out of the ordinary now. I thought all this as I knelt over Jim.

In the team I had one old horse that I knew could run. I put a saddle on her as quickly as I could, and put a bag across the front of the saddle as a cushion for Jim. I wrapped him in a blanket and climbed on to the horse with him.

The next minute we were racing down the steep hill, and we started our run. The horse was old and she breathed badly, but she loved to run and was the easiest horse I ever rode.

The bag fell on to the road, so I held Jim up to me like a baby the whole way. Even the strongest man will find it hard to hold a baby in one position for five minutes, but I never felt the ache in my arms that night. The Australian bush is always ghostly at night, and the moon played strange tricks. Roads through the bush made by the moonlight seemed straighter and clearer than the real one;

Roads through the bush made by the moonlight seemed straighter and clearer than the real one; you have to trust your horse then.

you have to trust your horse then. The bush seemed full of ghosts that night – all going my way and being left behind by the horse. Once I stopped to look at Jim. I just sat back and the horse slowed down. I felt Jim's hands: he was burning hot. I bent forwards and the horse began to run fast again. I kept saying out loud – and Mary and I often laughed about it (afterwards) – 'He's still limp! – Jim's still limp!' until the horse's feet echoed it. Then, just when I thought she was doing her best and racing her hardest, she suddenly started forwards. It was just what she'd do when I'd be riding alone and a strange horse came from behind. I *felt* the thing, too! I felt as if a strange horse *was* there! And then I started saying, 'Death is riding tonight! ... Death is racing tonight! ... Death is riding tonight!' till the horse's feet echoed that sound, too. And I believe the old horse felt the black horse at her side and was going to beat him or break her heart.

I was mad with fear and worry. I remember I kept saying, 'I'll be kinder to Mary after this! I'll spend more time with Jim!'

I don't know how the old horse got up the last hill, but I could see the house in front of me. It looked lonely in the moonlight: there were no lights on and I was very afraid that they had gone away. The horse stopped at the back of the house and someone shouted from inside, 'Who's there?'

'It's me, Joe Wilson. I want your sister-in-law – I've got the boy – he's sick and dying!'

Brighten came out, pulling up his trousers. 'What boy?' he asked.

'Here, take him,' I shouted, 'and let me get down.'

'What's the matter with him?' asked Brighten, and he seemed to hold back. Just as I went to get my leg over the saddle Jim's head went back over my arm, he went stiff, and I saw his eyes turn up and the whites shining in the moonlight.

I felt cold all over and sick in my stomach. I felt as if the worst had come. I wished it was all over and gone. I even thought about Mary and how we would bury Jim.

Then a woman ran out of the house. She put a hand on Jim, looked at his face, and then took him from me and ran into the kitchen, with me following her. By great good luck they had some dirty clothes on to boil in a bucket over the fire.

Brighten's sister-in-law dragged a large pot out from under the table and poured the hot water into it, clothes and all. Then she took a bucket of water from the corner and threw that in, and felt the water with her hand, holding Jim all the time. She stood him in the water and started wetting him all over, tearing off his clothes at the same time as she poured water on him.

It seemed to take for ever. And I? I felt as if I'd like to go outside until it was all over. I wished he was buried and it was all past. I felt – well, completely selfish. I only thought of myself.

Brighten's sister-in-law kept on working on Jim, and after about half an hour the end came: Jim went limp, he slipped down into the water and he was back in the world again.

I dropped on the chair by the table.

'It's all right,' she said. 'It's all over now. I wasn't going to let him die.'

I was only thinking, 'Well, it's over now, but it will come on again. I wish it was over for good. I'm tired of it.'

She called to her sister, Mrs Brighten, a helpless little fool of a woman, who'd been running in and out, 'Here, Jessie! Bring the new white blanket off my bed. And you, Brighten, take some of that wood off the fire and put something in that hole there to stop the wind.'

Brighten had been running in with sticks of wood. He took some of the wood outside, filled up the crack, and went inside and brought out a black bottle, got a cup from the cupboard and put both down by my elbow.

Mrs Brighten started to get some supper or breakfast, or whatever it was, ready. I didn't want to eat, so I sat and looked at

Brighten's sister-in-law. She was a big woman, her hands and feet were big, but they fitted her. She was a handsome woman – about forty, I should think. She had a square chin and a straight, thin-lipped mouth – straight except for a small turn down at the corners, which I imagined had been a sign of weakness in the days before she grew hard. There was no sign of weakness now. She had hard grey eyes and blue-black hair. She didn't ask me what happened to Jim, or how I got there, or who or what I was – at least not until the next night.

She sat up straight with Jim lying across her knees, held him gently and looked away into the past. Suddenly she looked round and said, as if I were her husband and she didn't think much of me, 'Why don't you eat something?'

'Beg pardon?'

'Eat something!'

I drank some tea and looked at her again. I was beginning to feel better, and I wanted Jim now that the colour was coming back into his face. I felt a lump rising in my throat and wanted to thank her. I took another look at her.

She was staring straight before her. I never saw a woman's face change so suddenly – and I never saw a woman's eyes so hopeless. Then I heard her take a long shaky breath, like an exhausted horse, and two great tears dropped from her wide-open eyes down her cheeks like raindrops on a face of stone. And in the firelight they seemed coloured by blood.

I looked away quickly, feeling full of tears myself. And she said, 'Go to bed.'

'Beg pardon?' (Her face was the same as before the tears.)

'Go to bed. There's a bed made for you inside on the sofa.'

'But – the horses – I must –'

'Brighen will ride down in the morning and look after them. Now you go to bed and get a good rest. The boy will be all right. I'll see to that.'

I went out — it was good to get out — to look at the horse I had ridden to Brighten's house. She couldn't eat yet, but just stood resting as best she could, with her nose over her food — and she breathed hard and sounded as though she was crying. I put my arms around her neck and I cried for the second time since I was a boy.

As I started to go in I heard Brighten's sister-in-law say, suddenly and sharply, 'Take *that* away, Jessie.'

And soon I saw Mrs Brighten go into the house with the black bottle. I looked through the kitchen window. Brighten's sister-in-law had moved away from the fire and sat near the table. She held Jim close as he slept.

I went to bed and slept until early the next afternoon. I woke up in time to hear the end of a conversation between Jim and Brighten's sister-in-law. He was asking her out to our place and she promised to come.

I never saw such a change in a woman as I saw in Brighten's sister-in-law that night. She was bright and cheerful, and seemed at least ten years younger. The table was set with the best glasses and plates, and she sat Jim in a chair and laughed and played with him like a great girl. She described Sydney and Sydney life as I'd never heard it described before; and she knew as much about the bush and the old gold-digging days as I did. She kept old Brighten and me talking and laughing until nearly midnight. And she seemed quick to understand everything when I talked. If she wanted to describe anything we hadn't seen, she could do it very clearly. A farmer with a very round, red face and a white hat had gone by that afternoon; she said it was 'like a mushroom on the rising moon'. She gave me a lot of good advice about children.

But she was quiet again next morning. She dressed Jim and gave him his breakfast, and made a comfortable place for him in the wagon. She got up on the wheel to do it herself. I'd half start to speak to her and then turn away and go fixing up round the horses, and then make another start to say goodbye. At last she took Jim into her arms and kissed him, and he put his arms tight round her neck and kissed her — a thing Jim seldom did with anybody except his mother.

'You'd better make a start,' she said. 'You want to get home early with that boy.'

I went round to where she stood. I held out my hand and tried to speak, but I could not.

'That's all right,' she said. Then tears came into her eyes and she suddenly put her hand on my shoulder and kissed me on the cheek. 'You be off — you're only a boy yourself. Take care of that boy; be kind to your wife, and take care of yourself.'

'Will you come to see us?'

'Some day,' she said.

I started the horses and looked round once more. She was looking up at Jim, and I saw that hungry, hopeless look come into her eyes.

I shortened the story when I told it to Mary — I didn't want to upset her. But, some time after I brought Jim home from Gulgong, and while I was at home with the team, Mary went over to visit Brighten's sister-in-law. It was a long way, so she stayed the night at Brighten's and came home the next afternoon. I was having a sleep on the sofa when she arrived, and the first thing I remember was someone stroking my head and kissing me, and I heard Mary saying, 'My poor boy! My poor old boy!'

I sat up quickly. I thought that Jim had gone off again. But it seems that Mary was only referring to me. Then she started pulling the grey hairs out of my head and putting them in an empty matchbox — to see how many she'd got. She used to do this when she was feeling a bit soft. I don't know what she said to Brighten's sister-in-law or what Brighten's sister-in-law said to her, but Mary was extra gentle for the next few days.

An Old-Time Episode in Tasmania

The view of Hobart Town from Cowa House was so beautiful people often stopped in surprise to admire it. The Derwent River curled slowly through Hobart Town, showing its brilliant blue in answer to the clear blue of the sky above. For all this the young man who held the horse's head outside Cowa House did not seem to care about the beauty which was before him. He was wearing the clothes of a working man, and indeed it was his job to look after both the horses and the gardens of his master's house. This in itself meant that his life had improved, for he was a convict who had nearly finished his time of imprisonment and so was allowed to work for a master away from the prison. Before, as a convict, he had been No. 213, and now he was a man with a name: Richard Cole. Yet still his life was hard and difficult, and even as he was thinking of his future he felt the sting of the whip on his face. He turned angrily to see who had hit him.

'Oh, please, I didn't mean it,' cried a little girl. 'I wanted to hit the flies on the horse's back. I hope I didn't hurt you.'

The man relaxed. Truca was nine, and the youngest daughter of his master, Wilfrid Paton. She sat now on the seat of the small cart behind the horse and looked at him with deep concern. His face changed to a broad smile and he took off his hat.

'Are you *talking* to the man, Truca?' cried a voice from the house. It made the little girl feel ashamed. 'What do you mean by disobeying orders, miss?'

The lady who came from the house looked as she sounded. She was a person who knew that she was always right, had always been right in the past and would always be right in the future. She knew the proper way to behave, and she knew even more clearly when people were not behaving properly. One understood at first sight that she was totally respectable and totally stiff; a closer inspection showed that she had been handsome, in a hard way, long before her niece was born. Indeed, Miss Paton looked very much as she was, hard and cold. Her brother, in contrast, was a handsome man who looked as though he might have too good a time, get drunk with his friends and sing 'I won't go home until morning.'

Although Wilfrid Paton was full of entertainment with his friends, he was firm and cruel with his convicts. He was part of a system designed to hold down the unhappy prisoners, and he could return easily to his breakfast or his dinner after seeing men flogged or even hanged. The position he held in the society of Tasmania took away his sense of the pain of the convicts; indeed, he divided the world into two parts, those who were convicts and those who were not. He thought about convicts in the same way as he thought about snakes: both were evil and less than human.

Miss Paton agreed with her brother's ideas. When Truca's mother died Wilfrid Paton had sent to England for his sister so that she could keep house for him. Miss Paton quickly took over and ran the house like a prison. She would not allow servants or children to disobey her orders. One of her firmest rules was that none of the Paton children should speak to a convict servant. It was very hard to follow this rule exactly, and Truca liked to talk to people, and it now seemed she would be punished.

Talking to the gardener was against the rules. Truca looked towards her approaching aunt, but Miss Paton hardly seemed to notice her.

'I suppose you will bring the woman back with you, Wilfrid?' she asked her brother. It was both a question and a command. 'Last time we had a woman who was drunk a lot of the time. Before that we had a thief. I really don't know which was worse. It is horrible to have to choose between evils, but I would almost suggest that you look among the – eh – child-killers this time.'

She turned her face away from Truca and the convict, afraid of saying 'child-killer' in front of them.

Mr Paton nodded. It was not the first time that she had sent him to choose a servant for her from the female prison. For some reason it would be difficult to explain, the people he chose were more likely to succeed than those chosen by his sister. Besides this, it was useful to have someone to blame when the servant failed to meet her demands.

The morning was beautiful. Truca was allowed to drive the horse, and she did it so well that her father settled back to smoke, and to think about a thousand things which it was perhaps better to leave alone. In certain moods he would wonder why he had ever come to this terrible part of the world. Talk about the convicts being in prison! What was he himself but a prisoner, since the day when he had madly decided to bring his family to Hobart Town, all because the pay of a Government clerk in England did not increase at the speed he needed it to. As a matter of fact he did not wear a prison uniform, and many people said that his home was in a most beautiful place, as close to heaven as one could ask. Still he felt he was a prisoner, and he would have given all the beauty here, and more besides, for a piece of London pavement in front of his old club. Mr Paton's world, indeed, was upset. Perhaps twelve years of accepting as normal the flogging and hanging of convicts had changed the way his mind worked. As for his happiness at home, he told himself that he had little to cheer about. His sister was cold and stubborn, and she was making his children, except perhaps Truca, follow her path.

Another problem was that in about a month's time Richard Cole would leave him and would again have his name and place in society; for Richard, who for the past five years had been No. 213, had nearly finished the time of his punishment. Richard had come to Tasmania as a convict because he had hit a man who swore to marry his sister whether she wished it or not. Unfortunately the blow was too hard and the man had died. His sister, who tried to save her brother by lying at his trial, was also found guilty, and was also transported to Australia as a convict. Nobody knew what had become of her. As far as Richard was concerned Mr Paton knew he did not want to lose such a good servant. It was very bad luck, Mr Paton thought, that he had found Richard so close to the end of his time. In fact, Richard had been so quiet and obedient that his time had been shortened as a reward, and Mr Paton felt cheated. As to keeping him after he was a free man, Mr Paton did not consider it. He was not used to the idea of free men as servants.

There was one way of keeping Richard as a convict, but it was a way even Mr Paton hesitated to employ. Richard had been able to obey almost impossible rules, and so had never been flogged; but if he was punished by a whipping, his time would be made longer and he would have to stay on as a convict servant with Mr Paton. All that was needed was a piece of paper in an envelope, which the victim himself carried to the nearest magistrate. Mr Paton would not have to give any reason for the flogging. Richard would be tied up and whipped, and any revenge would be impossible. Mr Paton did not really want to hurt him, but he was such a good servant, and perhaps he would be intelligent enough to understand that the nasty business of being flogged was really a sign of his master's concern, and indeed showed how much he was admired.

Truca's father was thinking this way when they arrived at the prison gate. It was a large bare building with white walls, standing in a place of amazing natural beauty. The little girl was allowed to go inside with her father while a man in a grey prison suit watched the horse.

Mr Paton had a difficult job. He was never gentle with convicts, male or female. He looked coldly at the women who were brought before him, all wearing the ugly prison uniform. Some looked at him in a half-friendly manner, but he turned away. After he had looked at all the women his choice seemed to be between a sour-looking older woman and a foolish, vacant girl. Then he saw a new face, a woman who stood out in the crowd like a sunny day in a month of bad weather.

'Who's that?' he asked.

'That's No. 27 – Amelia Clare – she came out in the last group.'

'Call her here, will you?'

In his early days Truca's father had been a great lover of Italian opera. As No. 27 came slowly towards him, something in her manner of walking and the expression in her beautiful grey eyes, reminded him of Amina in the *Somnambula*. The impression indeed was so strong that he would not have been surprised if she had begun to sing. He could have whistled the tune for her. Mr Paton reminded himself of why he was there and asked what work Amelia could do.

Amelia took a little time to reply, and when she did her voice was low and gentle. He found she was able to do fine sewing. 'I have forgotten so many things,' she sighed.

'We will give you a trial,' Mr Paton said, more gently than usual. 'I hope you won't regret it.'

When Amelia came back wearing her own clothes Mr Paton was surprised again. She looked like a lady, and a very pretty one at that. Her hair was roughly cut, but small curls still lay close to her head. She wore a very well-cut black jacket with a small hat. Mr Paton asked himself if he should take such a beauty home through the streets of Hobart Town. He noticed people turning to look at Amelia and he felt uneasy.

On their arrival at Cowa House the young gardener ran forward to open the gate; and here something unexpected happened. As Richard looked at the new servant he gave a sound and she looked round. Their eyes met and it was clear that they recognized each other immediately. Then they looked away and both looked as gloomy as before. Richard shut the gate carefully and Amelia stared at the clouds. Yet her employer had seen how she felt and it worried him. Who could tell what was happening? As No. 213 and No. 27 these two could have met before. Mr Paton believed that convicts had wonderful ways of making contact with each other. He also knew that young men and women can understand each other. He could not, however, decide why they had recognized each other so quickly, and rather hoped that it was simply because they were both convicts. He did not know how to handle matters of the heart. For some reason the thought of having Richard flogged was becoming more attractive. He put it away, angry with himself for even thinking about such a thing.

But the idea returned through the next few weeks, and was never stronger than when his little girl ran to him with a book in her hands.

'Oh, Papa, look! I've found someone just like Amelia in my picture-book. See? It's Snow White.* Only look, Papa!'

'Nonsense!' said her father, but he looked at the page. Truca was right. The picture had the eyes and mouth of Amelia Clare, frozen into beautiful stiffness. Mr Paton wished sometimes that he had not brought the girl into his house. Not that there was any kind of fault to be found with her. Even his sister, who demanded absolute obedience, could not complain about the new girl. Still, she upset the master of the house. If Richard's work seemed automatic, Amelia's seemed ghost-like, and when she moved noiselessly about the room he could not help following her uncomfortably with his eyes.

The days passed, each one like the one before it. December had come and gone. Mr Paton was between two devils, one of which

---

* Snow White. A person in a well-known children's story. She is very beautiful, and cannot wake up until the Prince kisses her.

whispered in his ear, 'Richard Cole is in love with No. 27. The time for him to be free is approaching. The first use he will make of it will be to leave you, and the next to marry Amelia Clare. You will lose everything at one blow. You will lose the best man-servant you have ever known, and your sister, the best girl. And more than this, you will lose an interest in life that gives it a taste and happiness it has not had for years. You wonder what secrets lie behind her face, and your heart beats more strongly and your blood runs more hotly. When this woman leaves, your life will become as dull as it was before.' To this devil Mr Paton replied strongly, 'I won't give the man the chance of marrying No. 27. As soon as he is free I will send him away and not let him return. As for Amelia, she is my prisoner, and I would send her back to prison tomorrow if I thought there was anything happening between them.'

At this point the second devil interrupted: 'There's a better way of arranging things. You can reduce Richard Cole in his own eyes and in the eyes of the girl he is after. The man is really very rude. It's just that he covers it up well, so you don't see it. Only make him angry enough and he'll make a mistake. A good flogging would set things right – you would keep your servant, and you would put a stop to this nonsense that is probably going on. But don't lose too much time; for if you wait until the last moment people will see what you are doing. The man is useful to him, they'll say, but it's rather hard on him to be like that.'

One evening in January, Mr Paton was supposed to be at his club. Instead he was seated in a bushy part of his garden, talking with his devils. The night had come down almost without his noticing – a night heavy with heat and blackness, and noisy with insects. Suddenly he heard a sound in the branches behind him. There was a light touch of hands on his shoulders and a soft face was laid against his cheeks. Two firm, warm lips pressed themselves on his, and a voice he recognized as Amelia's said, 'Dearest Dick, have I kept you waiting?'

There was a light touch of hands on his shoulders and a soft face was laid against his cheeks: 'Dearest Dick, have I kept you waiting?'

If anyone had suggested that he should change places with No. 213 he would have said that he would rather die first. But at this moment the convict's life seemed so much better than his own that he hardly dared to breathe so she would not find out who he was.

His silence worried her. 'Why don't you answer, Dick?' she asked impatiently.

'Answer? What am I to say?' replied her master. 'I'm not in the secret.'

Amelia did not give him time to say more. With a cry of terror she turned and ran, disappearing as quickly and mysteriously as she had come.

The words 'Dearest Dick' repeated themselves in Mr Paton's ears long after she had gone; and the more he heard them the more he felt tempted to give Richard a taste of the whip. He had tried unsuccessfully to anger the man into rudeness, but Richard remained obedient and polite. He gave his employer no chance to punish him, and if hit on one side of his face, he turned the other cheek. This had made his master extremely angry. But now at least Mr Paton felt he had reason to make an example of Richard Cole. He would teach the man to run after the woman convict behind his back! The devils persuaded Mr Paton so well that the next morning he felt he was absolutely right to call Richard to him after breakfast.

'Here,' he said, 'take this note over to Mr Merton and *wait for the answer.*'

There was nothing in this command to make the person receiving it turn pale. Richard had carried messages between his master and the magistrate at least twenty times before, and had thought nothing of it. But on this particular morning, as he took the note in his hands, he turned deathly white. Instead of taking it away quietly in his usual manner he fixed his eyes on his employer's face, and something in their expression actually made Mr Paton lower his own.

'May I speak a word with you, sir?' he said in a low, uncertain voice.

It was the first time that this had happened, and it seemed to Richard's master that the best way of meeting it would be to send the man away to do as he was told.

But Richard did not go. He stood for a moment with his head thrown back and the desperate look of a hunted animal in his eyes. At this moment a woman suddenly stepped between Mr Paton and his victim. Amelia was there, looking awake and alive as never before. She came close to her master – she had not spoken to him since the day she had entered his service – and raised her liquid eyes to his.

'You won't be hard on – my brother, sir, for the mistake I made last night?'

'Who said I was going to be hard on him?' asked Mr Paton, too surprised to think quickly. 'And if he's your brother, why do you wait until after dark to speak to him?'

Amelia did not move. 'Have I your permission to speak to him in the daytime, sir?' she asked.

'I'll think about all of this,' her master said. He turned to Richard. 'Get me the horse, and give me that note. I'll ride over with it myself.'

Three weeks later Richard Cole was a free man, and, within eight months of the day Mr Paton had driven Amelia Clare through the streets of Hobart Town to his house, she came politely to say goodbye. She was dressed in the same clothes as she had come in, but there was a big difference, for now she was free. He had a small number of coins for her and a little talk full of good advice, and so she was made ready to leave. He did not tell her that he would like her to stay. She controlled her own life now, as much or more so than the Queen of England herself, and it was not surprising if the first thing she did was to shake the dust of Cowa House off her feet. Still if she had only known, if she had only known. It seemed too hard to let her go with the knowledge that she never did or could know. Was it not for her that he had been the victim of his devils? For her that he so narrowly escaped being a criminal a while ago, and for her that he was now appearing as a kind changer of the convict system? He knew she would have understood him if she *had* known. But to explain was out of the question. He must tell either all or nothing, and the 'all' meant even more than he dared admit to himself.

This was why Amelia Clare left as she came, quietly and without telling any of her secrets. A fortnight after she had gone, as Mr Paton was gloomily smoking by his library fire in the early dark of a cold August evening, a letter was handed to him. The handwriting, very small and fine, was somehow familiar. He opened the letter and read:

Sir,

I want to tell you that I was married last week to Richard Cole, who was not my brother, as I led you to suppose, but my husband-to-be, for whom I would willingly again be unjustly transported. I believe that my lie saved Richard on at least one occasion. I trust you will pardon me.

Yours respectfully,
Amelia Cole

Mr Paton's kindness to his convict victims came to a sudden end. His behaviour became more cruel than ever before, and his name is remembered most unkindly in Tasmania.

ACTIVITIES

Dad and the Donovans

Before you read

1 Find these words in your dictionary:
   bark   paddock
   Write one sentence using both of these words.
2 This story is set in Queensland. What do you know about Queensland? Find out about its climate, land and cities.

After you read

3 Find examples of Dad's actions in the story to show that he is :
   a bad-tempered   **b** kind   **c** moral   **d** easy-going
4 Who are these people? Why are they important to the story?
   a Dave   **b** Old Anderson   **c** Red Donovan
   d Mick   **e** Joe   **f** the person telling the story
5 Work in pairs. Discuss which details in the story show how life for a small farmer in Australia a hundred years ago was more difficult than it is today.

The Ghost Upon the Rail

Before you read

6 Find these words in your dictionary:
   convict   handcuffs   magistrate   rail
   Which of these words are
   a people?   **b** made of metal?
   Write *two* sentences. Use *two* of the words in each sentence.
7 This is a partly true story about a famous Australian ghost. What famous ghost stories are there from your country? Do you believe in ghosts? Why, or why not?

After you read

8 Match the names of the characters from the story with the correct descriptions.
   a Ned Smith   is the first person to see the ghost.
   b John Fisher   is a policeman.

c Mr Dean   has not saved much money.

d David Weir   finds blood near the place where the ghost is seen.

e Mr Cox   has property in Sydney.

f Johnny Crook is a magistrate.

g Hamilton   is a barman.

9 Are these sentences true or false? Correct the false ones.

  a Fisher's ghost is wearing a hat.

  b It has not rained for a long time.

  c Three people see the ghost.

  d The dead body's pockets are empty.

  e Fisher was a generous man.

  f Most people think Smith is innocent of the murder.

  g The man who looks like Fisher helped Smith to plan the murder.

10 What do you think will happen to the man who helped Smith? If you were the judge, how would you punish him, and why?

The Dead Witness; or, the Bush Waterhole

Before you read

11 What special meaning does the word *bush* have in Australia?

12 What do you think the title means? Can a dead person be a witness?

After you read

13 What role do these play in helping Brooke to solve the crime?

  a Thomas Derrick   **b** Tom's animals   **c** a piece of glass

  d a photographic plate   **e** the rock water-hole

14 What is Dick's explanation for his sheep using the rock water-hole? How does Brooke know he is lying?

15 At the end of the story Brooke says that Dick was punished, but 'where and when it is unnecessary for me to say'. What does this suggest about Brooke's character, and what other details are there in the story to support your opinion?

Brighten's Sister-in-law

Before you read

16 Find these words in your dictionary.

convulsions limp saddle wagon

Which of these words refer to:

a a leather seat on a horse?

b violent and uncontrollable movements of the body?

c something without energy or strength?

d a type of transport?

Write *two* sentences. Use *all* of the words.

17 This story is about a child who has convulsions. Look at the picture on page 43. How do you think the parents are feeling? What would you do in that situation?

After you read

18 How many different types of work does Joe do in the story?

19 Joe and Mary's relationship is not easy. Find *five* examples in the story of when Joe and Mary think or act differently from each other.

20 Joe often says that his son is old for his age. What does he mean? Find examples in the story of Jim acting 'old for his age'.

21 A number of things about Jim's behaviour before he has a convulsion make Joe feel uneasy. What are they?

22 Why does Joe decide to take Jim to Brighten's place?

23 How does Brighten's sister-in-law change Joe and Mary's life?

An Old-Time Episode in Tasmania

Before you read

24 Find these words in your dictionary:

cart flog transport (v)

Write *one* sentence using all of the words.

25 This story is set in Tasmania. What do you know about Tasmania? Find it on a map.

After you read

26 What is Wilfrid Paton's relationship with

a Richard Cole?　　**b** Amelia Clare?

c Miss Paton? **d** his children?

How does he feel about them, and why?

27 What changes do the following things cause to Wilfrid Paton's life?

a living in Australia

b Amelia's arrival at Cowa House

c Amelia's letter

28 Work in pairs. Act out a conversation between Wilfrid Paton and Amelia Clare.

Student A: You are Wilfrid Paton. Try to persuade Amelia not to leave with her brother, but to stay with you as a housekeeper. Make your offer as attractive as possible (beautiful clothes, money, private rooms etc), but don't admit that you are in love her.

Student B: You are Amelia Clare. Politely refuse all of Wilfrid's wonderful offers, and give good reasons for refusing them. You don't want to make him angry, but don't tell him that you are not Richard's sister.

Writing

29 It's your job to encourage people to come and settle in Australia in the nineteenth century. Using information from these five stories, write a full page advertisement for an English newspaper, describing the attractions of life in Australia.

30 You are Ned Smith's lawyer. Write your speech for the judge, explaining why you think Smith is innocent, and why you think David Weir is the murderer.

31 You are Ned Smith. Write a full confession for the priest. Explain how and why you planned and carried out the murder, and how you made people believe that Fisher was in England.

32 Read page 54 again. Notice how 'She ... looked away into the past.' What do you think happened in the past to make Brighten's sister-in-law the way she is?

33 You are Richard Cole. Before Amelia comes to Cowa House, you write her a letter. Describe life at the house, and the people she will find there. Tell her your real feelings about Wilfrid Paton and his sister, and the way they treat you.

34 In 'The Ghost upon the Rail' and 'An Old-Time Episode in Tasmania', the rich people are all homesick for England. Have you ever felt homesick after being away from home for a long time? Write a report for a student magazine, describing your experience of being homesick. Describe how you felt, and what you did to make yourself feel better. Give advice to students who are about to live away from home for the first time.